FIRST 50 SONGS
YOU SHOULD PLAY ON THE BASS CLARINET

ISBN 978-1-5400-7005-0

Visit Hal Leonard Online at
www.halleonard.com

Contact us:
Hal Leonard
7777 West Bluemound Road
Milwaukee, WI 53213
Email: info@halleonard.com

In Europe, contact:
Hal Leonard Europe Limited
42 Wigmore Street
Marylebone, London, W1U 2RN
Email: info@halleonardeurope.com

In Australia, contact:
Hal Leonard Australia Pty. Ltd.
4 Lentara Court
Cheltenham, Victoria, 3192 Australia
Email: info@halleonard.com.au

ALL OF ME

BASS CLARINET

Words and Music by JOHN STEPHENS
and TOBY GAD

ALL YOU NEED IS LOVE

Bass Clarinet

Words and Music by JOHN LENNON
and PAUL McCARTNEY

AMAZING GRACE

BASS CLARINET

Traditional American Melody

BASIN STREET BLUES

Bass Clarinet

Words and Music by
SPENCER WILLIAMS

(small notes optional)

BEST SONG EVER

Bass Clarinet

Words and Music by EDWARD DREWETT,
WAYNE HECTOR, JULIAN BUNETTA
and JOHN RYAN

BEER BARREL POLKA
(Roll Out the Barrel)
Based on the European success "Skoda Lasky"*

BASS CLARINET

By LEW BROWN, WLADIMIR A. TIMM,
JAROMIR VEJVODA and VASEK ZEMAN

Polka tempo

CARNIVAL OF VENICE

BASS CLARINET

By JULIUS BENEDICT

CIRCLE OF LIFE

from THE LION KING

BASS CLARINET

Music by ELTON JOHN
Lyrics by TIM RICE

Moderately (with an African beat)

DOWN ON THE CORNER

BASS CLARINET

Words and Music by
JOHN FOGERTY

THE ELEPHANT
from CARNIVAL OF THE ANIMALS

BASS CLARINET

By CAMILLE SAINT-SAËNS

Allegretto pomposo

EVERMORE

from BEAUTY AND THE BEAST

BASS CLARINET

Music by ALAN MENKEN
Lyrics by TIM RICE

FLY ME TO THE MOON
(In Other Words)

Bass Clarinet

Words and Music by
BART HOWARD

FIGHT SONG

BASS CLARINET

Words and Music by RACHEL PLATTEN
and DAVE BASSETT

THE FOOL ON THE HILL

Words and Music by JOHN LENNON
and PAUL McCARTNEY

Bass Clarinet

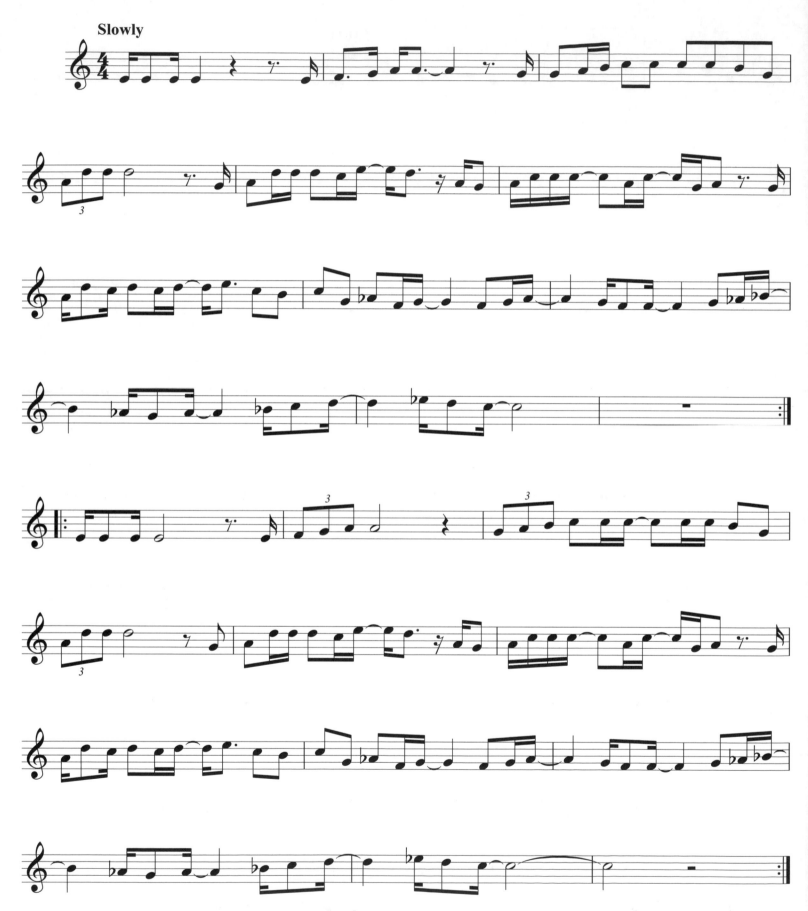

Slowly

GOD BLESS AMERICA®

BASS CLARINET

Words and Music by
IRVING BERLIN

THE GODFATHER
(Love Theme)
from the Paramount Picture THE GODFATHER

BASS CLARINET

By NINO ROTA

HALLELUJAH

Bass Clarinet

Words and Music by
LEONARD COHEN

HAPPY
from DESPICABLE ME 2

BASS CLARINET

Words and Music by
PHARRELL WILLIAMS

HELLO

BASS CLARINET

Words and Music by
LIONEL RICHIE

HELLO, DOLLY!

from HELLO, DOLLY!

BASS CLARINET

Music and Lyric by
JERRY HERMAN

HEY JUDE

BASS CLARINET

Words and Music by JOHN LENNON
and PAUL McCARTNEY

HOW DEEP IS YOUR LOVE

from the Motion Picture SATURDAY NIGHT FEVER

Bass Clarinet

Words and Music by BARRY GIBB,
ROBIN GIBB and MAURICE GIBB

I WILL ALWAYS LOVE YOU

BASS CLARINET

Words and Music by
DOLLY PARTON

Moderately slow

small notes optional

IN THE HALL OF THE MOUNTAIN KING

from PEER GYNT

BASS CLARINET

By EDVARD GRIEG

March tempo

THEME FROM "JAWS"

from the Universal Picture JAWS

Bass Clarinet

By JOHN WILLIAMS

Moderately

Repeat and Fade

JUST GIVE ME A REASON

Bass Clarinet

Words and Music by ALECIA MOORE,
JEFF BHASKER and NATE RUESS

CODA

JUST THE WAY YOU ARE

BASS CLARINET

Words and Music by BRUNO MARS,
ARI LEVINE, PHILIP LAWRENCE,
KHARI CAIN and KHALIL WALTON

LET IT GO
from FROZEN

BASS CLARINET

Music and Lyrics by KRISTEN ANDERSON-LOPEZ
and ROBERT LOPEZ

Slowly, in 2

LIVIN' ON A PRAYER

Bass Clarinet

Words and Music by JON BON JOVI,
DESMOND CHILD and RICHIE SAMBORA

MAS QUE NADA

BASS CLARINET

Words and Music by
JORGE BEN

MY HEART WILL GO ON
(Love Theme from 'Titanic')
from the Paramount and Twentieth Century Fox Motion Picture TITANIC

BASS CLARINET

Music by JAMES HORNER
Lyric by WILL JENNINGS

THE PINK PANTHER

from THE PINK PANTHER

Bass Clarinet

By HENRY MANCINI

NIGHT TRAIN

BASS CLARINET

Words by OSCAR WASHINGTON
and LEWIS C. SIMPKINS
Music by JIMMY FORREST

PETER GUNN
Theme Song from the Television Series

BASS CLARINET

By HENRY MANCINI

PURE IMAGINATION
from WILLY WONKA AND THE CHOCOLATE FACTORY

Bass Clarinet

Words and Music by LESLIE BRICUSSE
and ANTHONY NEWLEY

ROAR

BASS CLARINET

Words and Music by KATY PERRY,
MAX MARTIN, DR. LUKE,
BONNIE McKEE and HENRY WALTER

Moderately

ROLLING IN THE DEEP

BASS CLARINET

Words and Music by ADELE ADKINS
and PAUL EPWORTH

SATIN DOLL

BASS CLARINET

By DUKE ELLINGTON

SEE YOU AGAIN

from FURIOUS 7

Bass Clarinet

Words and Music by CAMERON THOMAZ,
CHARLIE PUTH, JUSTIN FRANKS,
ANDREW CEDAR, DANN HUME,
JOSH HARDY and PHOEBE COCKBURN

SHAKE IT OFF

Bass Clarinet

Words and Music by TAYLOR SWIFT,
MAX MARTIN and SHELLBACK

THE SORCERER'S APPRENTICE
(Theme)
from FANTASIA

Bass Clarinet

By PAUL DUKAS

STAND BY ME

Words and Music by JERRY LEIBER,
MIKE STOLLER and BEN E. KING

BASS CLARINET

THE STAR-SPANGLED BANNER

Bass Clarinet

Words by FRANCIS SCOTT KEY
Music by JOHN STAFFORD SMITH

STAY WITH ME

Bass Clarinet

Words and Music by SAM SMITH,
JAMES NAPIER, WILLIAM EDWARD PHILLIPS,
TOM PETTY and JEFF LYNNE

STOMPIN' AT THE SAVOY

Bass Clarinet

By BENNY GOODMAN,
EDGAR SAMPSON and CHICK WEBB

STRANGERS IN THE NIGHT

Bass Clarinet

Words by CHARLES SINGLETON and EDDIE SNYDER
Music by BERT KAEMPFERT

SUMMERTIME
from PORGY AND BESS®

BASS CLARINET

Music and Lyrics by GEORGE GERSHWIN,
DuBOSE and DOROTHY HEYWARD
and IRA GERSHWIN

THIS IS ME
from THE GREATEST SHOWMAN

Bass Clarinet

Words and Music by BENJ PASEK
and JUSTIN PAUL

UPTOWN FUNK

Bass Clarinet

Words and Music by MARK RONSON,
BRUNO MARS, PHILIP LAWRENCE, JEFF BHASKER, DEVON GALLASPY,
NICHOLAUS WILLIAMS, LONNIE SIMMONS, RONNIE WILSON,
CHARLES WILSON, RUDOLPH TAYLOR and ROBERT WILSON

WHAT A WONDERFUL WORLD

Bass Clarinet

Words and Music by GEORGE DAVID WEISS
and BOB THIELE